Best-Loved PSALMS

Best-Loved
Psalms

Clare Haworth-Maden
Editor

Barnes
&Noble
BOOKS
NEW YORK

Page 1: King David, as envisaged by Peter Paul Rubens (1577–1640). Seventy-three Psalms are specifically associated with David, himself a legendary poet and musician.

Page 2: A northern European depiction of an angelic choir praising God with a variety of instruments, in accordance with the exhortation in Psalm 150.

Page 3: Angels are usually depicted as messengers of God.

This edition published by Barnes and Noble, Inc., by arrangement with Saraband Inc.

Design © Ziga Design
Editor: Clare Haworth-Maden

Library of Congress Cataloging in Publication Data available

ISBN: 0-7607-0805-3

Printed in China

10 9 8 7 6 5 4 3 2

Acknowledgements
Extracts from the Authorized Version of the Bible (The King James Bible), the rights in which are vested in the Crown, are reproduced by permission of the Crown's Patentee, Cambridge University Press.

The publisher would like to thank the following people for their assistance in the preparation of this book: Clare Haworth-Maden, editor; Nicola Gillies, art editor; Wendy J. Ciaccia, graphic designer. Grateful acknowledgement is also made for the illustrations featured in this book, which are reproduced by courtesy of Planet Art and CorelDraw, except those on pages 35 and 54, which are courtesy of Saraband Image Library.

*This volume is dedicated to the
Reverend Canon Godfrey Hirst*

Contents

Introduction

P aeans of praise; wretched, heart-rending laments; glowing affirmations of belief; or comforting words of solace—the poetic resonance of the Psalms of ancient Israel echoes down the centuries, retaining its power to move and inspire us. The Psalms are often set to music (like Psalm 23, "The Lord is my shepherd"), or better known as hymns (such as Luther's version of Psalm 46, "God is our refuge and strength"), and even those who do not read the scriptures or worship formally in Christian churches or Jewish synagogues are familiar with the elegiac words of at least one of the Psalms: the most famous of all, Psalm 23.

What Are the Psalms?

The Book of Psalms is a collection of sacred songs contained in the Old Testament, appearing between the Book of Job and Proverbs. Important as the Psalms are in the rites and belief of Christianity, in Judaism they are even more significant, for they formed part of the sacred, musical rituals of worship of the ancient Temple. Indeed, the word "psalm" derives from the Greek *psalmos*, meaning "a song accompanied by a harp," which itself evolved from the verb *psallein*—"to play the harp." Furthermore, the alternative name of the Book of Psalms is the psaltery (from the Greek *psalterion*, which signifies a stringed musical instrument). In Hebrew, however, the Psalms are termed the *Tehillîm*, translated as "the book of praises."

Prior to the groundbreaking theological research of the twentieth century, which was aided by such archaeological finds as the Dead Sea Scrolls, it was believed that the Psalms dated from the Maccabean-Hasmonean period (168–34 BC); it is now thought that they are of a considerably earlier date.

The Psalms and Biblical History

Although 49 of the Psalms are anonymous, many are preceded in the text by explanatory phrases that were inserted later (probably during the Hellenic period), such as "Psalm of David." This attribution is popularly interpreted to mean that David—a poet, musician, and founder of the guilds of Temple singers and musicians—was the author of the Psalm. However, modern theologians believe that the Psalm is an evocation of, or dedication to David, or that it concerns him. There are 73 Davidic Psalms. Other individuals specified include the (unnamed) chief musician of the period; Solomon (two Psalms); Moses (one); the wise men and Temple musicians Heman and Ethan the Ezrahite (one each); the Levite Asaph (12); and such collectives as the Temple singers called the "sons of Korah" (12).

Other terms included in prefatory texts, such as "Gittith" or "Maschil," refer to musical instructions. In the case of David, certain Psalms refer to specific incidents in his life

Below: Gustave Doré (1832–83) depicts the young David clinging to his harp as he is threatened by Saul; Psalms 54 and 57 are among those that refer to David's flight from the jealous king.

(confirmed in the First Book of Samuel): Psalms 54 and 57, for example, recall respectively David's exposure by the Ziphites and his flight from Saul. Other Psalms can also be firmly linked to Biblical events. They include the evocative and well-known Psalm 137, "By the rivers of Babylon," which refers to the bitterness of the Babylonian Exile; Psalm 74, "O God, why hast thou cast us off for ever?," which describes the destruction of the Temple; and Psalm 114, "When Israel went out of Egypt," which tells of God's deliverance of the Israelites from slavery.

The Significance of the Psalms in Judaic Worship

It is believed that the Psalms were first written for liturgical use in the Temple—the focus of Jewish religious life—and that they were performed during the period of the Second Temple (Zerubbabel's, c. 520–20 BC; rebuilt by Herod the Great, c. 19 BC, and destroyed AD 70). The fact that 148 Asaphites and other lay singers were among those who returned from the Babylonian Exile, as stated in the Bible, indicates that the Psalms were also sung during the period of the First Temple (Solomon's, c. 950–587 BC).

The musical terms contained in the descriptive phrases preceding certain Psalms indicate how they should be performed, with regard to the use of certain ancient and prescribed melodies, or of specific instruments. Unfortunately, the exact significance of these terms, and the way in which they should be applied, has been lost in the mists of time.

In Hebrew worship, some Psalms were reserved for certain occasions: Psalms 113–118, for example, known as the "*Hallel*" (praise) Psalms, were recited during the Passover, while the various "Songs of Degrees/Ascents" were sung by pilgrims ascending to Jerusalem.

Composition and Arrangement of the Psalms

The Book of Psalms, which comprises 150 Psalms, is divided into five books: Book I (numbers 1–41); Book II (42–72); Book III (73–89); Book IV (90–106); and Book V (107–150). Since there is a certain amount of "crossover"—repetition of verses—across the various books, it is believed that they were once separate entities. This assumption is strengthened by the appearance of a doxology (a formal expression of praise) at the end of each book: the last verse of Psalm 89 at the end of Book III, for example, reads "Blessed be the LORD for evermore. Amen, and Amen." Psalm 150—the last one—can be regarded as a doxology in itself.

The composition of each Psalm adheres to the principles of Hebrew poetry, each line expanding on the content of the previous verse. Some, including Psalms 25, 111 and 145, are acrostic: that is, each line or verse begins with a consecutive letter of the Hebrew alphabet. Psalm 119 is the most elaborate example of this pattern of composition.

As a result of the pioneering work of the theologian Hermann Gunkel, in terms of content, the Psalms can be roughly grouped into four main categories: first, joyful hymns in praise of God (such as Psalms 8, 19 and 104; the "songs of Zion," including Psalms 46 and 48; and "enthronement Psalms," such as Psalm 47); secondly, royal Psalms (including Psalms 2, 21 and 45); thirdly, individual, collective and national laments (such as Psalms 6, 22, 25, 38, 74, 85 and 88); and lastly, individual and collective thanksgiving (including Psalms 32, 40, 66 and 118). Other groupings may also be identified, but they have gained less general acceptance among theologians: wisdom Psalms (such as Psalm 32), and liturgical Psalms (including 1, 15, 25, 32, 40, 85 and 114). However, such classification should be regarded only as a guide to the reader, for many Psalms overlap the categories, or can be interpreted in different ways.

Left: The advent of a messiah is believed to be the subject of seventeen Psalms, according to Christian interpretation. Here, the adoration of the newly born Christ is sensitively depicted by Velázquez (1599–1660).

The "Messianic" Psalms

A group of 17 Psalms has particular significance in Christian belief. Psalms 2, 8, 16, 22, 40, 41, 45, 68, 69, 72, 78, 89, 102, 109, 110, 118 and 132) appear to refer to the coming of the messiah, although it is believed that this was not the intention of the composer, who was simply describing the reigning king. In Judaism, the messiah has yet to be manifested, but Christians, of course, believe that Jesus Christ is the messiah evoked by the Psalms. Indeed, the Gospel writers of the New Testament quoted selected phrases contained in the "messianic" Psalms and put them into Jesus' mouth, thus apparently confirming his role as the messiah. In Psalm 2, for example, the Lord states: "Thou art my Son; this day have I begotten thee" (compare with Acts 13:33). Verse 21 of Psalm 69, "They gave me also gall for my meat; and in my thirst they gave me vinegar to drink" (compare with Matthew 27:34, 48), seems to predict the Crucifixion; while Psalm 22 contains not only Christ's words on the cross, "My God, my God, why hast thou forsaken me?" (compare with Matthew 27:46), but also the verse "They part my garments among them, and cast lots upon my vesture" (compare with John 19:24), as well as "they pierced my hands and feet."

The Selection of Psalms in This Book

The Psalms selected include the best known, but they also provide a balanced representation of all the categories discussed above. An abbreviated reference to those categories that apply appears at the foot of each Psalm. The text is taken from the King James Bible (the Authorized Version, 1611), the most poetic of the English translations.

In the words of the noted British theological writer C.S. Lewis : "The Psalms are poems, and poems intended to be sung: not doctrinal treatises, nor even sermons…They must be read as poems if they are to be understood." Whether or not the reader is familiar with the Judeo-Christian tradition, he or she will be inspired and uplifted by the profound wisdom, feeling and faith expressed by the Psalmists.

BOOK I

⟨∽νννν∾⟩

PSALM 1

1. Blessed *is* the man that walketh not in the counsel of the ungodly, nor standeth in the way of sinners, nor sitteth in the seat of the scornful.
2. But his delight *is* in the law of the LORD; and in his law doth he meditate day and night.
3. And he shall be like a tree planted by the rivers of water, that bringeth forth his fruit in season; his leaf also shall not wither; and whatsoever he doeth shall prosper.
4. The ungodly *are* not so; but *are* like the chaff which the wind driveth away.
5. Therefore the ungodly shall not stand in the judgment, nor sinners in the congregation of the righteous.
6. For the LORD knoweth the way of the righteous; but the way of the ungodly shall perish.

—WISDOM

PSALM 2

1. Why do the heathen rage, and the people imagine a vain thing?
2. The kings of the earth set themselves, and the rulers take counsel together, against the LORD, and against his anointed, *saying,*
3. Let us break their bands asunder, and cast away their cords from us.
4. He that sitteth in the heavens shall laugh: the Lord shall have them in derision.
5. Then shall he speak unto them in his wrath, and vex them in his sore displeasure.
6. Yet I have set my king upon my holy hill of Zion.
7. I will declare the decree: the LORD hath said unto me, Thou *art* my Son; this day have I begotten thee.

8   Ask of me, and I shall give *thee* the heathen *for* thine inheritance, and the uttermost parts of the earth *for* thy possession.

9   Thou shalt break them with a rod of iron; thou shalt dash them in pieces like a potter's vessel.

10 Be wise now therefore, O ye kings: be instructed, ye judges of the earth.

11 Serve the LORD with fear, and rejoice with trembling.

12 Kiss the Son, lest he be angry, and ye perish *from* the way, when his wrath is kindled but a little. Blessed *are* all they that put their trust in him.

—ROYAL, MESSIANIC

Left: *The enthroned Christ—an image from the fifteenth-century book of hours,* Les Très Riches Heures du Duc de Berry. *Christians believe that certain Psalms, such as Psalm 2, prophesy the life of their messiah.*

Right: *Many Psalms are poetical laments appealing to God for solace; in this detail from a painting by Dante Gabriel Rossetti (1828–82), God's angelic messenger appears to console one such troubled soul.*

Psalm 4

To the chief Musician on Negonith,
A Psalm of David.

1   Hear me when I call, O God of my righteousness: thou hast enlarged me *when I was* in distress; have mercy upon me, and hear my prayer.

2   O ye sons of men, how long *will ye turn* my glory into shame? *how long* will ye love vanity, *and* seek after leasing? Selah.

3   But know that the Lord hath set apart him that is godly for himself: the Lord will hear when I call unto him.

4   Stand in awe, and sin not: commune with your own heart upon your bed, and be still. Selah.

5   Offer the sacrifices of righteousness, and put your
trust in the Lᴏʀᴅ.

6   *There be* many that say, Who will shew us *any* good?
Lᴏʀᴅ, lift thou up the light of thy countenance
upon us.

7   Thou has put gladness in my heart, more than in the
time *that* their corn and their wine increased.

8   I will both lay me down in peace and sleep: for thou,
Lᴏʀᴅ, only makest me dwell in safety.

           —Dᴀᴠɪᴅɪᴄ, ʟᴀᴍᴇɴᴛ, ᴛʜᴀɴᴋsɢɪᴠɪɴɢ

Psᴀʟᴍ 6

To the chief Musician on Neginoth upon
Sheminith, A Psalm of David.

1   O Lᴏʀᴅ, rebuke me not in thine anger, neither
chasten me in thy hot displeasure.

2   Have mercy upon me, O Lᴏʀᴅ; for I *am* weak: O
Lᴏʀᴅ, heal me; for my bones are vexed.

3   My soul is also sore vexed: but thou, O Lᴏʀᴅ, how long?

4   Return, O Lᴏʀᴅ, deliver my soul: oh save me for thy
mercies' sake.

5   For in death *there is* no remembrance of thee: in the
grave who shall give thee thanks?

6   I am weary with my groaning; all the night make I
my bed to swim; I water my couch with my tears.

7   Mine eye is consumed because of grief; it waxeth old
because of all mine enemies.

8   Depart from me, all ye workers of iniquity; for the
Lᴏʀᴅ hath heard the voice of my weeping.

9   The Lᴏʀᴅ hath heard my supplication; the Lᴏʀᴅ will
receive my prayer.

10 Let all mine enemies be ashamed and sore vexed: let
them return *and* be ashamed suddenly.

                  —Dᴀᴠɪᴅɪᴄ, ʟᴀᴍᴇɴᴛ

PSALM 15

A Psalm of David.

Below: God Creates the Sun and the Moon *(1511)—a detail from Michelangelo's Sistine Chapel ceiling. Verses 4 to 6 of Psalm 19 describe the Sun's splendid strength but, as verse 1 stresses, this mighty astral body is but the "handywork" of God.*

1   Lord, who shall abide in thy tabernacle? who shall dwell in thy holy hill?

2   He that walketh uprightly, and worketh righteousness, and speaketh the truth in his heart.

3   *He that* backbiteth not with his tongue, nor doeth evil to his neighbour, nor taketh up a reproach against his neighbour.

4   In whose eyes a vile person is condemned; but he honoureth them that fear the LORD. *He that* sweareth to *his own* hurt, and changeth not.

5   *He that* putteth not out his money to usury, nor taketh reward against the innocent. He that doeth these *things* shall never be moved.

—DAVIDIC, WISDOM

PSALM 19

To the chief Musician, A Psalm of David.

1   The heavens declare the glory of God; and the
    firmament sheweth his handywork.
2   Day unto day uttereth speech, and night unto night
    sheweth knowledge.
3   *There is* no speech nor language, *where* their voice is
    not heard.
4   Their line is gone out through all the earth, and their
    words to the end of the world. In them hath he set a
    tabernacle for the sun.
5   Which *is* as a bridegroom coming out of his chamber,
    and rejoiceth as a strong man to run a race.
6   His going forth *is* from the end of the heaven, and his
    circuit unto the ends of it: and there is nothing hid
    from the heat thereof.
7   The law of the LORD *is* perfect, converting the soul: the
    testimony of the LORD *is* sure, making wise the simple.
8   The statutes of the LORD *are* right, rejoicing the heart: the
    commandment of the LORD *is* pure, enlightening the eyes.
9   The fear of the LORD *is* clean, enduring for ever: the
    judgments of the LORD *are* true *and* righteous altogether.
10 More to be desired *are they* than gold, yea, than much fine
    gold: sweeter also than honey and the honeycomb.
11 Moreover by them is thy servant warned: *and* in
    keeping of them *there is* great reward.
12 Who can understand *his* errors? cleanse thou me
    from secret *faults.*
13 Keep back thy servant also from presumptuous *sins;*
    let them not have dominion over me: then shall I be
    upright, and I shall be innocent from the great
    transgression.
14 Let the words of my mouth, and the meditation of
    my heart, be acceptable in thy sight, O LORD, my
    strength, and my redeemer.

                                        —DAVIDIC, PRAISE

PSALM 21

To the chief Musician, A Psalm of David.

1 The king shall joy in thy strength, O Lord; and in thy salvation how greatly shall he rejoice!

2 Thou hast given him his heart's desire and hast not withholden the request of his lips. Selah.

3 For thou preventest him with the blessings of goodness: thou settest a crown of pure gold on his head.

4 He asked life of thee, *and* thou gavest *it* him, *even* length of days for ever and ever.

5 His glory *is* great in thy salvation: honour and majesty hast thou laid upon him.

6 For thou hast made him most blessed for ever: thou hast made him exceedingly glad with thy countenance.

7 For the king trusteth in the Lord, and through the mercy of the most High he shall not be moved.

8 Thine hand shall find out all thine enemies: thy right hand shall find out those that hate thee.

9 Thou shalt make them as a fiery oven in the time of thine anger: the Lord shall swallow them up in his wrath, and the fire shall devour them.

10 Their fruit shalt thou destroy from the earth, and their seed from among the children of men.

11 For they intended evil against thee: they imagined a mischievous device, *which* they are not able *to perform*.

12 Therefore shalt thou make them turn their back, *when* thou shalt make ready *thine arrows* upon thy strings against the face of them.

13 Be thou exalted, Lord, in thine own strength; *so* will we sing and praise thy power.

—DAVIDIC, ROYALTY

PSALM 22

*To the chief Musician upon Aijeleth Shahar,
A Psalm of David.*

1 My God, my God, why hast thou forsaken me? *why
art thou so* far from helping me, *and from* the words
of my roaring?

2 O my God, I cry in the daytime, but thou hearest not;
and in the night season, and am not silent.

3 But thou *art* holy, *O thou* that inhabitest the praises
of Israel.

4 Our fathers trusted in thee: they trusted, and thou
didst deliver them.

5 They cried unto thee, and were delivered: they
trusted in thee, and were not confounded.

6 But I *am* a worm, and no man; a reproach of men,
and despised of the people.

7 All they that see me laugh me to scorn: they shoot
out the lip, they shake the head, *saying,*

8 He trusted on the LORD *that* he would deliver him: let
him deliver him, seeing he delighted in him.

9 But thou *art* he that took me out of the womb: thou didst
make me hope *when I was* upon my mother's breasts.

10 I was cast upon thee from the womb: thou *art* my
God from my mother's belly.

11 Be not far from me; for trouble *is* near; for *there is*
none to help.

12 Many bulls have compassed me: strong *bulls* of
Bashan have beset me round.

13 They gaped upon me *with* their mouths, *as* a
ravening and a roaring lion.

14 I am poured out like water, and all my bones are out
of joint: my heart is like wax; it is melted in the midst
of my bowels.

15 My strength is dried up like a potsherd; and my
tongue cleaveth to my jaws; and thou hast brought
me into the dust of death.

*Below: The praying
hands so masterfully
engraved by Albrecht
Dürer (1471–1528)
eloquently express the
plea for God's help
expressed in Psalm
22:19— "Be not thou
far from me, O LORD:
O my strength, haste
thee to help me."*

Opposite: *Raphael's Crucifixion (1503)* *recalls the words that, according to Matthew 27:46, the dying Christ uttered on the cross: "My God, my God, why hast thou forsaken me?" These also constitute the opening lines of Psalm 22, thereby underlining its significance to Christians as a messianic Psalm.*

16 For dogs have compassed me: the assembly of the wicked have inclosed me: they pierced my hands and my feet.

17 I may tell all my bones: they look *and* stare upon me.

18 They part my garments among them, and cast lots upon my vesture.

19 But be not thou far from me, O Lord: O my strength, haste thee to help me.

20 Deliver my soul from the sword; my darling from the power of the dog.

21 Save me from the lion's mouth: for thou hast heard me from the horns of the unicorns.

22 I will declare thy name unto my brethren: in the midst of the congregation will I praise thee.

23 Ye that fear the Lord, praise him; all ye the seed of Jacob, glorify him; and fear him, all ye the seed of Israel.

24 For he hath not despised nor abhorred the affliction of the afflicted; neither hath he hid his face from him; but when he cried unto him, he heard.

25 My praise *shall be* of thee in the great congregation: I will pay my vows before them that fear him.

26 The meek shall eat and be satisfied: they shall praise the Lord that seek him: your heart shall live for ever.

27 All the ends of the world shall remember and turn unto the Lord: and all the kindreds of the nations shall worship before thee.

28 For the kingdom *is* the Lord's: and he *is* the governor among the nations.

29 All *they that be* fat upon earth shall eat and worship: all they that go down to the dust shall bow before him: and none can keep alive his own soul.

30 A seed shall serve him; it shall be accounted to the Lord for a generation.

31 They shall come, and shall declare his righteousness unto a people that shall be born, that he hath done *this*.

—Davidic, lament, messianic

PSALM 23

A Psalm of David.

1   The LORD *is* my shepherd; I shall not want.
2   He maketh me to lie down in green pastures:
he leadeth me beside the still waters.
3   He restoreth my soul: he leadeth me in the paths
of righteousness for his name's sake.
4   Yea, though I walk through the valley of the shadow
of death, I will fear no evil: for thou *art* with me; thy
rod and thy staff they comfort me.
5   Thou preparest a table before me in the presence of
mine enemies: thou anointest my head with oil; my
cup runneth over.
6   Surely goodness and mercy shall follow me all the
days of my life: and I will dwell in the house of the
LORD for ever.

—DAVIDIC, THANKSGIVING, LITURGY

PSALM 25

A Psalm of David.

1   Unto thee, O LORD, do I lift up my soul.
2   O my God, I trust in thee: let me not be ashamed, let
not mine enemies triumph over me.
3   Yea, let none that wait on thee be ashamed: let them
be ashamed which transgress without cause.
4   Shew me thy ways, O LORD; teach me thy paths.
5   Lead me in thy truth, and teach me: for thou *art* the
God of my salvation; on thee do I wait all the day.
6   Remember, O LORD, thy tender mercies and thy
lovingkindnesses; for they *have been* ever of old.
7   Remember not the sins of my youth, nor my
transgressions: according to thy mercy remember
thou me for thy goodness' sake, O LORD.

8 Good and upright is the LORD: therefore will he teach sinners in the way.

9 The meek will he guide in judgment: and the meek will he teach his way.

10 All the paths of the LORD *are* mercy and truth unto such as keep his covenant and his testimonies.

11 For thy name's sake, O LORD, pardon mine iniquity; for it *is* great.

12 What man *is* he that feareth the LORD? him shall he teach in the way *that* he shall choose.

13 His soul shall dwell at ease; and his seed shall inherit the earth.

14 The secret of the LORD *is* with them that fear him; and he will shew them his covenant.

15 Mine eyes *are* ever toward the LORD; for he shall pluck my feet out of the net.

16 Turn thee unto me, and have mercy upon me; for I *am* desolate and afflicted.

17 The troubles of my heart are enlarged: O bring thou me out of my distresses.

18 Look upon mine affliction and my pain; and forgive all my sins.

19 Consider mine enemies; for they are many; and they hate me with cruel hatred.

20 O keep my soul, and deliver me: let me not be ashamed; for I put my trust in thee.

21 Let integrity and uprightness preserve me; for I wait on thee.

22 Redeem Israel, O God, out of all his troubles.

—DAVIDIC, LAMENT, ACROSTIC

Below: *A king prays devoutly before an altar in an image drawn from* Les Très Riches Heures du Duc de Berry *(a book of hours). The humble monarch David pleads that God should "Remember not the sins of my youth, nor my transgressions…" in Psalm 25:7.*

PSALM 27

A Psalm of David.

1 The LORD *is* my light and my salvation; whom shall I fear? the LORD *is* the strength of my life; of whom shall I be afraid?

2 When the wicked, *even* mine enemies and my foes, came upon me to eat up my flesh, they stumbled and fell.

3 Though an host should encamp against me, my heart shall not fear: though war should rise against me, in this *will* I *be* confident.

4 One *thing* have I desired of the LORD, that will I seek after; that I may dwell in the house of the LORD all the days of my life, to behold the beauty of the LORD, and to enquire in his temple.

5 For in the time of trouble he shall hide me in his pavilion: in the secret of his tabernacle shall he hide me; he shall set me up upon a rock.

6 And now shall mine head be lifted up above mine enemies round me: therefore will I offer in his tabernacle sacrifices of joy; I will sing, yea, I will sing praises unto the LORD.

7 Hear, O LORD, *when* I cry with my voice: have mercy also upon me, and answer me.

8 *When thou saidst,* Seek ye my face; my heart said unto thee, Thy face, LORD, will I seek.

9 Hide not thy face *far* from me; put not thy servant away in anger: thou hast been my help; leave me not, neither forsake me, O God of my salvation.

10 When my father and my mother forsake me, then the LORD will take me up.

11 Teach me thy way, O LORD, and lead me in a plain path, because of mine enemies.

12 Deliver me not over unto the will of mine enemies: for false witnesses are risen up against me, and such as breathe out cruelty.

13 *I had fainted*, unless I had believed to see the
    goodness of the LORD in the land of the living.
14 Wait on the LORD: be of good courage, and he shall
    strengthen thine heart: wait, I say, on the LORD.
                    —DAVIDIC, LAMENT, THANKSGIVING

PSALM 32

A Psalm of David, Maschil.

1 Blessed *is he whose* transgression *is* forgiven, *whose* sin *is* covered.

2 Blessed *is* the man unto whom the LORD imputeth not iniquity, and in whose spirit *there is* no guile.

3 When I kept silence, my bones waxed old through my roaring all the day long.

4 For day and night thy hand was heavy upon me: my moisture is turned into the drought of summer. Selah.

5 I acknowledged my sin unto thee, and mine iniquity have I not hid. I said, I will confess my transgressions unto the LORD; and thou forgavest the iniquity of my sin. Selah.

6 For this shall every one that is godly pray unto thee in a time when thou mayest be found: surely in the floods of great waters they shall not come nigh unto him.

7 Thou *art* my hiding place; thou shalt preserve me from trouble; thou shalt compass me about with songs of deliverance. Selah.

8 I will instruct thee and teach thee in the way which thou shalt go: I will guide thee with mine eye.

9 Be ye not as the horse, *or* as the mule, *which* have no understanding: whose mouth must be held in with bit and bridle, lest they come near unto thee.

10 Many sorrows *shall be* to the wicked: but he that trusteth in the LORD, mercy shall compass him about.

11 Be glad in the LORD, and rejoice, ye righteous: and shout for joy, all *ye that are* upright in heart.

—DAVIDIC, WISDOM

Below: Psalm 32:9 condemns the horse and mule in allegorical terms, both for their lack of intelligence and their innate tendency to attack the hand that restrains them, and urges humanity to rise above its animal nature and accept God's enlightenment.

PSALM 38

A Psalm of David, to bring to remembrance.

1   O LORD, rebuke me not in thy wrath: neither chasten me in thy hot displeasure.

2   For thine arrows stick fast in me, and thy hand presseth me sore.

3   *There is* no soundness in my flesh because of thine anger; neither *is there any* rest in my bones because of my sin.

4   For mine iniquities are gone over mine head: as an heavy burden they are too heavy for me.

5   My wounds stink *and* are corrupt because of my foolishness.

6   I am troubled; I am bowed down greatly; I go mourning all the day long.

7   For my loins are filled with a loathsome *disease*: and *there is* no soundness in my flesh.

8   I am feeble and sore broken: I have roared by reason of the disquietness of my heart.

9   Lord, all my desire *is* before thee; and my groaning is not hid from thee.

10 My heart panteth, my strength faileth me: as for the light of mine eyes, it also is gone from me.

11 My lovers and my friends stand aloof from my sore; and my kinsmen stand afar off.

12 They also that seek after my life lay snares *for me*: and they that seek my hurt speak mischievous things, and imagine deceits all the day long.

13 But I, as a deaf *man*, heard not; and *I was* as a dumb man *that* openeth not his mouth.

14 Thus I was as a man that heareth not, and in whose mouth *are* no reproofs.

15 For in thee, O LORD, do I hope: thou wilt hear, O Lord my God.

16 For I said, *Hear me*, lest *otherwise* they should rejoice over me: when my foot slippeth, they magnify *themselves* against me.

Below: Abraham prepares to sacrifice his beloved son in The Sacrifice of Isaac *by Caravaggio (1571–1610) before God causes his hand to be stayed, for: "sacrifice and offering thou didst not desire…" (Psalm 40:6).*

17 For I *am* ready to halt, and my sorrow *is* continually before me.

18 For I will declare mine iniquity; I will be sorry for my sin.

19 But mine enemies *are* lively, *and* they are strong: and they that hate me wrongfully are multiplied.

20 They also that render evil for good are mine adversaries; because I follow *the thing that* good *is.*

21 Forsake me not, O LORD: O my God, be not far from me.

22 Make haste to help me, O Lord my salvation.

—DAVIDIC, LAMENT, PRAISE

Psalm 40

To the chief Musician, A Psalm of David.

1 I waited patiently for the Lord; and he inclined unto me, and heard my cry.

2 He brought me up also out of an horrible pit, out of the miry clay, and set my feet upon a rock, *and* established my goings.

3 And he hath put a new song in my mouth, *even* praise unto our God: many shall see *it*, and fear, and shall trust in the Lord.

4 Blessed *is* that man that maketh the Lord his trust, and respecteth not the proud, nor such as turn aside to lies.

5 Many, O Lord my God, *are* thy wonderful works *which* thou hast done, and thy thoughts *which are* to us-ward: they cannot be reckoned up in order unto thee: *if* I would declare and speak *of them*, they are more than can be numbered.

6 Sacrifice and offering thou didst not desire; mine ears hast thou opened: burnt offering and sin offering hast thou not required.

7 Then said I, Lo, I come: in the volume of the book *it is* written of me.

8 I delight to do thy will, O my God: yea, thy law *is* within my heart.

9 I have preached righteousness in the great congregation: lo, I have not refrained my lips, O Lord, thou knowest.

10 I have not hid thy righteousness within my heart; I have declared thy faithfulness and thy salvation: I have not concealed thy lovingkindness and thy truth from the great congregation.

11 Withhold not thou thy tender mercies from me, O Lord: let thy lovingkindness and thy truth continually preserve me.

12 For innumerable evils have compassed me about: mine iniquities have taken hold upon me, so that I

am not able to look up; they are more than the hairs of mine head: therefore my heart faileth me.

13 Be pleased, O LORD, to deliver me: O LORD, make haste to help me.

14 Let them be ashamed and confounded together that seek after my soul to destroy it: let them be driven backward and put to shame that wish me evil.

15 Let them be desolate for a reward of their shame that say unto me, Aha, aha.

16 Let all those that seek thee rejoice and be glad in thee: let such as love thy salvation say continually, The LORD be magnified.

17 But I *am* poor and needy; *yet* the Lord thinketh upon me: thou *art* my help and my deliverer; make no tarrying, O my God.

—DAVIDIC, THANKSGIVING, MESSIANIC

Right: *St. John the Evangelist— accompanied by his symbolic attribute, the eagle—in exile on the Island of Patmos, in* Les Très Riches Heures du Duc de Berry. *St. John occasionally drew upon the words of the Psalms when composing his gospel.*

BOOK II

⚮

PSALM 45

*To the chief Musician upon Shoshannim, for the sons of
Korah, Maschil, A Song of loves.*

*Previous page: The
chalices this angel
carries have various
significances in the
Bible. They may
represent God's blessing
and the spiritual
riches that true faith
brings, as described
in Psalm 45.*

1 My heart is inditing a good matter: I speak of the
things which I have made touching the king: my
tongue *is* the pen of a ready writer.

2 Thou art fairer than the children of men: grace is
poured into thy lips: therefore God hath blessed thee
for ever.

3 Gird thy sword upon *thy* thigh, O *most* mighty, with
thy glory and thy majesty.

4 And in thy majesty ride prosperously because of
truth and meekness *and* righteousness; and thy right
hand shall teach thee terrible things.

5 Thine arrows *are* sharp in the heart of the king's
enemies; *whereby* the people fall under thee.

6 Thy throne, O God, *is* for ever and ever: the sceptre of
thy kingdom *is* a right sceptre.

7 Thou lovest righteousness, and hatest wickedness:
therefore God, thy God, hath anointed thee with the
oil of gladness above thy fellows.

8 All thy garments *smell* of myrrh, and aloes, *and*
cassia, out of the ivory palaces, whereby they have
made thee glad.

9 Kings' daughters *were* among thy honourable
women: upon thy right hand did stand the queen in
gold of Ophir.

10 Hearken, O daughter, and consider, and incline thine
ear; forget also thine own people, and thy father's house;

11 So shall the king greatly desire thy beauty: for he *is*
thy Lord; and worship thou him.

12 And the daughter of Tyre *shall be there* with a gift;
even the rich among the people shall entreat thy
favour.

13 The king's daughter *is* all glorious within: her
clothing *is* of wrought gold.

14 She shall be brought unto the king in raiment of needlework: the virgins her companions that follow her shall be brought unto thee.

15 With gladness and rejoicing shall they be brought: they shall enter into the king's palace.

16 Instead of thy fathers shall be thy children, whom thou mayest make princes in all the earth.

17 I will make thy name to be remembered in all generations: therefore shall the people praise thee for ever and ever.

—ROYALTY, MESSIANIC, PRAISE

Below: This painting in the Christian "throne of grace" style represents God supporting the crucified Christ, above whose head hovers the dove that represents the Holy Spirit. "Thy throne, O God is for ever and ever…" (Psalm 45:6).

PSALM 46

To the chief Musician for the sons of Korah,
A Song upon Alamoth.

1   God *is* our refuge and strength, a very present help in
     trouble.
2   Therefore will not we fear, though the earth be
     removed, and though the mountains be carried into
     the midst of the sea;
3   *Though* the waters thereof roar *and* be troubled,
     though the mountains shake with the swelling
     thereof. Selah.
4   *There is* a river, the streams whereof shall make glad
     the city of God, the holy *place* of the tabernacles of
     the most High.
5   God *is* in the midst of her; she shall not be moved:
     God shall help her, *and that* right early.
6   The heathen raged, the kingdoms were moved: he
     uttered his voice, the earth melted.
7   The Lord of hosts *is* with us; the God of Jacob *is* our
     refuge. Selah.
8   Come, behold the works of the Lord, what
     desolations he hath made in the earth.
9   He maketh wars to cease unto the end of the earth;
     he breaketh the bow, and cutteth the spear in sunder;
     he burneth the chariot in the fire.
10   Be still, and know that I *am* God; I will be exalted
     among the heathen, I will be exalted in the earth.
11   The Lord of hosts *is* with us; the God of Jacob *is* our
     refuge. Selah.

—PRAISE, THANKSGIVING

PSALM 47

To the chief Musician, A Psalm for the sons of Korah.

1 O clap your hands, all ye people; shout unto God with the voice of triumph.

2 For the LORD most high *is* terrible; *he is* a great King over all the earth.

3 He shall subdue the people under us, and the nations under our feet.

4 He shall choose our inheritance for us, the excellency of Jacob whom he loved. Selah.

5 God is gone up with a shout, the LORD with the sound of a trumpet.

6 Sing praises to God, sing praises: sing praises unto our King, sing praises.

7 For God *is* the King of all the earth: sing ye praises with understanding.

8 God reigneth over the heathen: God sitteth upon the throne of his holiness.

9 The princes of the people are gathered together, *even* the people of the God of Abraham: for the shields of the earth *belong* unto God: he is greatly exalted.

—LITURGY, ROYALTY, PRAISE

Left: "Be still, and know that I am God" (Psalm 46:10). Here, His power is revealed to the Pharaoh, as promised to Moses, when Aaron's staff changes into a serpent.

PSALM 48

A Song and Psalm for the sons of Korah.

1 Great *is* the LORD, and greatly to be praised in the city of our God, *in* the mountain of his holiness.

2 Beautiful for situation, the joy of the whole earth, *is* mount Zion, *on* the sides of the north, the city of the great King.

3 God is known in her palaces for a refuge.

4 For, lo, the kings were assembled, they passed by together.

5 They saw *it, and so* they marvelled; they were troubled, *and* hasted away.

6 Fear took hold upon them there, *and* pain, as of a woman in travail.

7 Thou breakest the ships of Tarshish with an east wind.

8 As we have heard, so have we seen in the city of the LORD of hosts, in the city of our God: God will establish it for ever. Selah.

9 We have thought of thy lovingkindness, O God, in the midst of thy temple.

10 According to thy name, O God, so *is* thy praise unto the ends of the earth: thy right hand is full of righteousness.

11 Let mount Zion rejoice, let the daughters of Judah be glad, because of thy judgments.

12 Walk about Zion, and go round about her: tell the towers thereof.

13 Mark ye well her bulwarks, consider her palaces; that ye may tell *it* to the generation following.

14 For this God *is* our God for ever and ever: he will be our guide *even* unto death.

—LITURGY, PRAISE

PSALM 54

To the chief Musician on Neginoth, Maschil,
A Psalm of David, when the Ziphims came and said
to Saul, Doth not David hide himself with us?

Below: *Arms piously crossed, a kneeling king pleads for God's mercy and salvation, as expressed in Psalms 54 and 57, which refer to the exiled David during his flight from Saul.*

1 Save me, O God, by thy name, and judge me by thy strength.

2 Hear my prayer, O God; give ear to the words of my mouth.

3 For strangers are risen up against me, and oppressors seek after my soul: they have not set God before them. Selah.

4 Behold, God *is* mine helper: the Lord *is* with them that uphold my soul.

5 He shall reward evil unto mine enemies: cut them off in thy truth.

6 I will freely sacrifice unto thee; I will praise thy name, O LORD; for *it is* good.

7 For he hath delivered me out of all trouble: and mine eye hath seen *his desire* upon mine enemies.

—DAVIDIC, LAMENT

PSALM 57

To the chief Musician, Al-taschith, Michtam of David, when he fled from Saul in the cave.

1 Be merciful unto me, O God, be merciful unto me: for my soul trusteth in thee: yea, in the shadow of thy wings will I make my refuge, until *these* calamities be overpast.

2 I will cry unto God most high; unto God that performeth *all things* for me.

3 He shall send from heaven, and save me *from* the reproach of him that would swallow me up. Selah. God shall send forth his mercy and his truth.

4 My soul *is* among lions: *and* I lie *even among* them that are set on fire, *even* the sons of men, whose teeth *are* spears and arrows, and their tongue a sharp sword.

5 Be thou exalted, O God, above the heavens; *let* thy glory *be* above all the earth.

6 They have prepared a net for my steps; my soul is bowed down: they have digged a pit before me, into the midst whereof they are fallen *themselves*. Selah.

7 My heart is fixed, O God, my heart is fixed: I will sing and give praise.

8 Awake up, my glory; awake, psaltery and harp: I *myself* will awake early.

9 I will praise thee, O Lord, among the people: I will sing unto thee among the nations.

10 For thy mercy *is* great unto the heavens, and thy truth unto the clouds.

11 Be thou exalted, O God, above the heavens: *let* thy glory *be* above all the earth.

—DAVIDIC, LAMENT, PRAISE

Opposite: *A detail from William Morris's stained-glass window in the Church of St. Peter and St. Paul, Cattistock, England (1882). "Awake up, my glory; awake, psaltery and harp:…I will praise thee, O Lord, among the people:" (Psalm 57:8–9).*

PSALM 66

To the chief Musician, A Song or Psalm.

1   Make a joyful noise unto God, all ye lands;

2   Sing forth the honour of his name: make his praise glorious.

3   Say unto God, How terrible *art thou in* thy works! through the greatness of thy power shall thine enemies submit themselves unto thee.

4   All the earth shall worship thee, and shall sing unto thee; they shall sing *to* thy name. Selah.

5   Come and see the works of God: *he is* terrible *in his* doing toward the children of men.

6   He turned the sea into dry *land*: they went through the flood on foot: there did we rejoice in him.

7   He ruleth by his power for ever; his eyes behold the nations: let not the rebellious exalt themselves. Selah.

8   O bless our God, ye people, and make the voice of his praise to be heard:

9   Which holdeth our soul in life, and suffereth not our feet to be moved.

10 For thou, O God, hast proved us: thou hast tried us, as silver is tried.

11 Thou broughtest us into the net; thou laidst affliction upon our loins.

12 Thou hast caused men to ride over our heads; we went through fire and through water: but thou broughtest us out into a wealthy *place*.

13 I will go into thy house with burnt offerings: I will pay thee my vows,

14 Which my lips have uttered, and my mouth hath spoken, when I was in trouble.

15 I will offer unto thee burnt sacrifices of fatlings, with the incense of rams; I will offer bullocks with goats. Selah.

16 Come *and* hear, all ye that fear God, and I will declare what he hath done for my soul.

17 I cried unto him with my mouth, and he was extolled with my tongue.

18 If I regard iniquity in my heart, the Lord will not hear *me*:

19 *But* verily God hath heard *me*; he hath attended to the voice of my prayer.

20 Blessed *be* God, which hath not turned away my prayer, nor his mercy from me.

—LITURGY, PRAISE, THANKSGIVING

Left: *Many Psalms, including Psalm 66:1— "Make a joyful noise unto God…"—exhort the worship of God through the medium of music, and in artistic representations, angels are frequently depicted making music in glorification of the Lord.*

Psalm 68

To the chief Musician, A Psalm or Song of David.

Below: A detail from Michelangelo's The Flood, *painted on the ceiling of the Sistine Chapel, graphically illustrates how God metes out punishment to those who "hate him" (Psalm 68:1); by contrast, verse 9 describes how a merciful God sent rain to bring relief to his people's parched land.*

1 Let God arise, let his enemies be scattered: let them also that hate him flee before him.

2 As smoke is driven away, *so* drive *them* away: as wax melteth before the fire, *so* let the wicked perish at the presence of God.

3 But let the righteous be glad; let them rejoice before God: yea, let them exceedingly rejoice.

4 Sing unto God, sing praises to his name: extol him that rideth upon the heavens by his name JAH, and rejoice before him.

5 A father of the fatherless, and a judge of the widows, *is* God in his holy habitation.

6 God setteth the solitary in families: he bringeth out those which are bound with chains: but the rebellious dwell in a dry *land.*

7 O God, when thou wentest forth before thy people, when thou didst march through the wilderness; Selah:

8 The earth shook, the heavens also dropped at the presence of God: *even* Sinai itself *was moved* at the presence of God, the God of Israel.

9 Thou, O God, didst send a plentiful rain, whereby thou didst confirm thine inheritance, when it was weary.

10 Thy congregation hath dwelt therein: thou, O God, hast prepared of thy goodness for the poor.

11 The Lord gave the word: great *was* the company of those that published *it.*

12 Kings of armies did flee apace: and she that tarried at home divided the spoil.

13 Though ye have lien among the pots, *yet shall ye be as* the wings of a dove covered with silver, and her feathers with yellow gold.

14 When the Almighty scattered kings in it, it was *white* as snow in Salmon.

15 The hill of God *is as* the hill of Bashan; an high hill *as* the hill of Bashan.

16 Why leap ye, ye high hills? *this is* the hill *which* God desireth to dwell in; yea, the LORD will dwell *in it* for ever.

17 The chariots of God *are* twenty thousand, *even* thousands of angels: the Lord is among them, *as in* Sinai, in the holy *place*.

18 Thou hast ascended on high, thou hast led captivity captive: thou hast received gifts for men; yea, *for* the rebellious also, that the LORD God might dwell *among them*.

19 Blessed *be* the Lord, *who* daily loadeth us *with benefits, even* the God of our salvation. Selah.

20 *He that is* our God *is* the God of salvation; and unto GOD the Lord *belong* the issues from death.

21 But God shall wound the head of his enemies, *and* the hairy scalp of such an one as goeth on still in his trespasses.

22 The Lord said, I will bring again from Bashan, I will bring *my people* again from the depths of the sea:

23 That thy foot may be dipped in the blood of *thine* enemies, *and* that the tongue of thy dogs in the same.

24 They have seen thy goings, O God; *even* the goings of my God, my King, in the sanctuary.

25 The singers went before, the players on instruments *followed* after; among *them were* the damsels playing with timbrels.

26 Bless ye God in the congregations, *even* the Lord, from the fountain of Israel.

Below: As the messengers of God, angels actively defend the faith against evil-doers on the Lord's behalf, for: "God shall wound the head of his enemies…" (Psalm 68:21).

27 There *is* little Benjamin *with* their ruler, the princes of Judah *and* their council, the princes of Zebulun, *and* the princes of Naphtali.

28 Thy God hath commanded thy strength: strengthen, O God, that which thou hast wrought for us.

29 Because of thy temple at Jerusalem shall kings bring presents unto thee.

30 Rebuke the company of spearmen, the multitude of the bulls, with the calves of the people, *till every one* submit himself with pieces of silver: scatter thou the people *that* delight in war.

31 Princes shall come out of Egypt; Ethiopia shall soon stretch out her hands unto God.

32 Sing unto God, ye kingdoms of the earth; O sing praises unto the Lord. Selah:

33 To him that rideth upon the heavens of heavens, *which were* of old; lo, he doth send out his voice, *and that* a mighty voice.

34 Ascribe ye strength unto God: his excellency *is* over Israel, and his strength *is* in the clouds.

35 O God, *thou art* terrible out of thy holy places: the God of Israel *is* he that giveth strength and power unto *his* people. Blessed *be* God.

—DAVIDIC, LITURGY, PRAISE, MESSIANIC

PSALM 69

To the chief Musician upon Shoshannim,
A Psalm of David.

1 Save me, O God; for the waters are come in unto
my soul.

2 I sink in deep mire, where *there is* no standing:
I am come into deep waters, where the floods
overflow me.

3 I am weary of my crying: my throat is dried: mine
eyes fail while I wait for my God.

4 They that hate me without a cause are more than the
hairs of mine head: they that would destroy me, *being*
mine enemies wrongfully, are mighty: then I restored
that which I took not away.

5 O God, thou knowest my foolishness; and my sins are
not hid from thee.

6 Let not them that wait on thee, O Lord GOD of
hosts, be ashamed for my sake: let not those that seek
thee be confounded for my sake, O God of Israel.

7 Because for thy sake I have borne reproach; shame
hath covered my face.

8 I am become a stranger unto my brethren, and an
alien unto my mother's children.

9 For the zeal of thine house hath eaten me up; and the
reproaches of them that reproached thee are fallen
upon me.

10 When I wept, *and chastened* my soul with fasting, that
was to my reproach.

11 I made sackcloth also my garment; and I became a
proverb to them.

12 They that sit in the gate speak against me; and I *was*
the song of the drunkards.

13 But as for me, my prayer *is* unto thee, O LORD, *in* an
acceptable time: O God, in the multitude of thy
mercy hear me, in the truth of thy salvation.

14   Deliver me out of the mire, and let me not sink: let me be delivered from them that hate me, and out of the deep waters.

15   Let not the waterflood overflow me, neither let the deep swallow me up, and let not the pit shut her mouth upon me.

16   Hear me, O LORD; for thy lovingkindness *is* good: turn unto me according to the multitude of thy tender mercies.

17   And hide not thy face from thy servant; for I am in trouble: hear me speedily.

18   Draw nigh unto my soul, *and* redeem it: deliver me because of mine enemies.

19   Thou hast known my reproach, and my shame, and my dishonour: mine adversaries *are* all before thee.

20   Reproach hath broken my heart; and I am full of heaviness: and I looked *for some* to take pity, but *there was* none; and for comforters, but I found none.

21   They gave me also gall for my meat; and in my thirst they gave me vinegar to drink.

22   Let their table become a snare before them: and *that which should have been* for *their* welfare, *let it become* a trap.

23   Let their eyes be darkened, that they see not; and make their loins continually to shake.

24   Pour out thine indignation upon them, and let thy wrathful anger take hold of them.

25   Let their habitations be desolate: *and* let none dwell in their tents.

26   For they persecute *him* whom thou hast smitten; and they talk to the grief of those whom thou hast wounded.

27   Add iniquity unto their iniquity: and let them not come into thy righteousness.

28   Let them be blotted out of the book of the living, and not be written with the righteous.

29 But I *am* poor and sorrowful: let thy salvation, O God, set me up on high.

30 I will praise the name of God with a song, and will magnify him with thanksgiving.

31 *This* also shall please the LORD better than an ox *or* bullock that hath horns and hoofs.

32 The humble shall see *this, and* be glad: and your heart shall live that seek God.

33 For the LORD heareth the poor, and despiseth not his prisoners.

34 Let the heaven and earth praise him, the seas, and every thing that moveth therein.

35 For God will save Zion, and will build the cities of Judah: that they may dwell there, and have it in possession.

36 The seed also of his servants shall inherit it: and they that love his name shall dwell therein.

—DAVIDIC, LAMENT, MESSIANIC

Below: *Velázquez's painting of 1628 anticipates Christ's crucifixion. The words of Psalm 69:21—"They gave me also gall for meat and in my thirst they gave me vinegar to drink"—are also attributed to Christ in his death throes (Matthew 27:34,48).*

PSALM 70

To the chief Musician, A Psalm of David,
to bring to remembrance.

1   Make haste, O God, to deliver me; make haste to help
     me, O Lord.
2   Let them be ashamed and confounded that seek after
     my soul; let them be turned backward, and put to
     confusion, that desire my hurt.
3   Let them be turned back for a reward of their shame
     that say, Aha, aha.
4   Let all those that seek thee rejoice and be glad in thee;
     and let such as love thy salvation say continually, Let
     God be magnified.
5   But I am poor and needy; make haste unto me, O
     God: thou art my help and my deliverer; O LORD,
     make no tarrying.

—DAVIDIC, LAMENT

*Right: Paul, under
attack by an angry
crowd while preaching
in Jerusalem, praying
for deliverance—the
theme of Psalm 70.
Paul was saved from
the rioters by Roman
soldiers, who
imprisoned him but
later released him
unharmed.*

BOOK III

∽〰〰〰

PSALM 74

Maschil of Asaph.

Previous page:
*In Christian belief,
the annunciation of
her impending
motherhood was made
to Mary by Gabriel.
In this depiction, the
archangel's messenger
carries a staff that has
assumed the form of a
lily, representing
Mary's purity.*

1   O God, why hast thou cast *us* off for ever? *why* doth thine anger smoke against the sheep of thy pasture?

2   Remember thy congregation, *which* thou hast purchased of old; the rod of thine inheritance, *which* thou hast redeemed; this mount Zion, wherein thou hast dwelt.

3   Lift up thy feet unto the perpetual desolations; *even* all *that* the enemy hath done wickedly in the sanctuary.

4   Thine enemies roar in the midst of thy congregations; they set up their ensigns *for* signs.

5   A *man* was famous according as he had lifted up axes upon the thick trees.

6   But now they break down the carved work thereof at once with axes and hammers.

7   They have cast fire into thy sanctuary, they have defiled *by casting down* the dwelling place of thy name to the ground.

8   They said in their hearts, Let us destroy them together: they have burned up all the synagogues of God in the land.

9   We see not our signs: *there is* no more any prophet: neither *is there* among us any that knoweth how long.

10   O God, how long shall the adversary reproach? shall the enemy blaspheme thy name for ever?

11   Why withdrawest thou thy hand, even thy right hand? pluck *it* out of thy bosom.

12   For God *is* my King of old, working salvation in the midst of the earth.

13   Thou didst divide the sea by thy strength: thou brakest the heads of the dragons in the waters.

14   Thou brakest the heads of leviathan in pieces, *and* gavest him *to be* meat to the people inhabiting the wilderness.

15 Thou didst cleave the fountain and the flood: thou driedst up mighty rivers.

16 The day *is* thine, the night also *is* thine: thou hast prepared the light and the sun.

17 Thou hast set all the borders of the earth: thou hast made summer and winter.

18 Remember this, *that* the enemy hath reproached, O LORD, and *that* the foolish people have blasphemed thy name.

19 O deliver not the soul of thy turtledove unto the multitude *of the wicked*: forget not the congregation of thy poor for ever.

20 Have respect unto the covenant: for the dark places of the earth are full of the habitations of cruelty.

21 O let not the oppressed return ashamed: let the poor and needy praise thy name.

22 Arise, O God, plead thine own cause: remember how the foolish man reproacheth thee daily.

23 Forget not the voice of thine enemies: the tumult of those that rise up against thee increaseth continually.

—LITURGY, LAMENT

Below: The grief of the prophet Jeremiah, as interpreted by Michelangelo in a Sistine Chapel fresco. Jeremiah witnessed the destruction of the First Temple (Solomon's) by the Babylonians in 587 BC, an event that is bitterly lamented in Psalm 74.

PSALM 85

To the chief Musician, A Psalm for the sons of Korah.

1 LORD, thou hast been favourable unto thy land: thou hast brought back the captivity of Jacob.

2 Thou hast forgiven the iniquity of thy people, thou hast covered all their sin. Selah.

3 Thou hast taken away all thy wrath: thou hast turned *thyself* from the fierceness of thine anger.

4 Turn us, O God of our salvation, and cause thine anger toward us to cease.

5 Wilt thou be angry with us for ever? wilt thou draw out thine anger to all generations?

6 Wilt thou not revive us again: that thy people may rejoice in thee?

7 Shew us thy mercy, O LORD, and grant us thy salvation.

8 I will hear what God the LORD will speak: for he will speak peace unto his people, and to his saints: but let them not turn again to folly.

9 Surely his salvation *is* nigh them that fear him; that glory may dwell in our land.

10 Mercy and truth are met together; righteousness and peace have kissed *each other.*

11 Truth shall spring out of the earth; and righteousness shall look down from heaven.

12 Yea, the LORD shall give *that which is* good; and our land shall yield her increase.

13 Righteousness shall go before him; and shall set *us* in the way of his steps.

—LITURGY, LAMENT, PRAISE

Below: *Both Psalms 74 and 85 request a renewal of God's covenant with the people of Israel. A dove bearing an olive branch, symbolic of this renewal, carried God's message to Noah after the flood; and in Psalm 74:19, the Israelites are compared with "the soul of thy turtledove."*

PSALM 88

*A Song or Psalm for the sons of Korah,
to the chief Musician upon Mahalath Leannoth,
Maschil of Heman the Ezrahite.*

1 O LORD God of my salvation, I have cried day *and* night before thee:

2 Let my prayer come before thee: incline thine ear unto my cry;

3 For my soul is full of troubles: and my life draweth nigh unto the grave.

4 I am counted with them that go down into the pit: I am as a man *that hath* no strength:

5 Free among the dead, like the slain that lie in the grave, whom thou rememberest no more: and they are cut off from thy hand.

6 Thou hast laid me in the lowest pit, in darkness, in the deeps.

7 Thy wrath lieth hard upon me, and thou hast afflicted *me* with all thy waves. Selah.

8 Thou hast put away mine acquaintance far from me; thou hast made me an abomination unto them: *I am* shut up, and I cannot come forth.

9 Mine eye mourneth by reason of affliction: LORD, I have called daily upon thee, I have stretched out my hands unto thee.

10 Wilt thou shew wonders to the dead? shall the dead arise *and* praise thee? Selah.

11 Shall thy lovingkindness be declared in the grave? *or* thy faithfulness in destruction?

12 Shall thy wonders be known in the dark? and thy righteousness in the land of forgetfulness?

13 But unto thee have I cried, O LORD; and in the morning shall my prayer prevent thee.

14 LORD, why casteth thou off my soul? *why* hidest thou thy face from me?

15 I *am* afflicted and ready to die from my youth up: *while* I suffer thy terrors I am distracted.

16 Thy fierce wrath goeth over me; thy terrors have cut me off.

17 They came round about me daily like water; they compassed me about together.

18 Lover and friend hast thou put far from me, *and* mine acquaintance into darkness.

—LITURGY, LAMENT

Right: William Blake's The Ancient of Days *(1794) envisages God engaged in the act of creation. Psalm 89:11 celebrates the Lord's omnipotence with such verses as "The heavens are* thine, the earth also is *thine: as* for the *world and the fulness thereof, thou hast founded them…."*

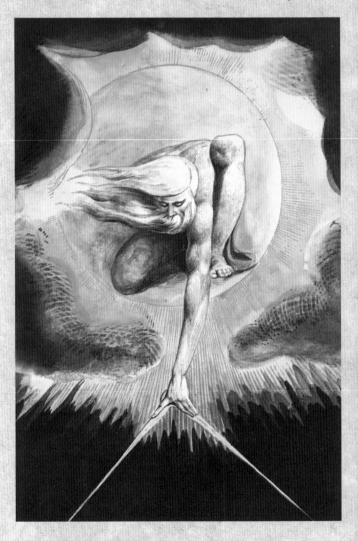

PSALM 89

Maschil of Ethan the Ezrahite.

1 I will sing of the mercies of the LORD for ever: with my mouth will I make known thy faithfulness to all generations.

2 For I have said, Mercy shall be built up for ever: thy faithfulness shalt thou establish in the very heavens.

3 I have made a covenant with my chosen, I have sworn unto David my servant,

4 Thy seed will I establish for ever, and build up thy throne to all generations. Selah.

5 And the heavens shall praise thy wonders, O LORD: thy faithfulness also in the congregation of the saints.

6 For who in the heaven can be compared unto the LORD? *who* among the sons of the mighty can be likened unto the LORD?

7 God is greatly to be feared in the assembly of the saints, and to be had in reverence of all *them that are* about him.

8 O Lord God of hosts, who *is* a strong LORD like unto thee? or to thy faithfulness round about thee?

9 Thou rulest the raging of the sea: when the waves thereof arise, thou stillest them.

10 Thou hast broken Rahab in pieces, as one that is slain; thou hast scattered thine enemies with thy strong arm.

11 The heavens *are* thine, the earth also *is* thine: *as for* the world and the fulness thereof, thou hast founded them.

12 The north and the south thou hast created them: Tabor and Hermon shall rejoice in thy name.

13 Thou hast a mighty arm: strong is thy hand, *and* high is thy right hand.

14 Justice and judgment *are* the habitation of thy throne: mercy and truth shall go before thy face.

15 Blessed *is* the people that know the joyful sound: they shall walk, O LORD, in the light of thy countenance.

16 In thy name shall they rejoice all the day: and in thy righteousness shall they be exalted.

17 For thou *art* the glory of their strength: and in thy favour our horn shall be exalted.

18 For the LORD *is* our defence; and the Holy One of Israel *is* our king.

19 Then thou spakest in vision to thy holy one, and saidst, I have laid help upon *one that is* mighty; I have exalted *one* chosen out of the people.

20 I have found David my servant; with my holy oil have I anointed him:

21 With whom my hand shall be established: mine arm also shall strengthen him.

22 The enemy shall not exact upon him; nor the son of wickedness afflict him.

23 And I will beat down his foes before his face, and plague them that hate him.

24 But my faithfulness and my mercy *shall be* with him: and in my name shall his horn be exalted.

25 I will set his hand also in the sea, and his right hand in the rivers.

26 He shall cry unto me, Thou *art* my father, my God, and the rock of my salvation.

27 Also I will make him *my* first-born, higher than the kings of the earth.

28 My mercy will I keep for him for evermore, and my covenant shall stand fast with him.

29 His seed also will I make *to endure* for ever, and his throne as the days of heaven.

30 If his children forsake my law, and walk not in my judgments;

31 If they break my statutes, and keep not my commandments;

32 Then will I visit their transgression with the rod, and their iniquity with stripes.

33 Nevertheless my lovingkindness will I not utterly take from him, nor suffer my faithfulness to fail.

34 My covenant will I not break, nor alter the thing that is gone out of my lips.

35 Once have I sworn by my holiness that I will not lie unto David.

36 His seed shall endure for ever, and his throne as the sun before me.

37 It shall be established for ever as the moon, and *as* a faithful witness in heaven. Selah.

38 But thou hast cast off and abhorred, thou hast been wroth with thine anointed.

Left: *Moses bearing the Tablets of the Decalogue on Mount Sinai. Psalm 89:30–32 recalls God's warning that the Ten Commandments, inscribed on the Tablets given to Moses, must be obeyed.*

39 Thou hast made void the covenant of thy servant: thou hast profaned his crown *by casting it* to the ground.

40 Thou hast broken down all his hedges; thou hast brought his strong holds to ruin.

41 All that pass by the way spoil him: he is a reproach to his neighbours.

42 Thou hast set up the right hand of his adversaries; thou hast made all his enemies to rejoice.

43 Thou hast also turned the edge of his sword, and hast not made him to stand in the battle.

44 Thou hast made his glory to cease, and cast his throne down to the ground.

45 The days of his youth hast thou shortened: thou hast covered him with shame. Selah.

46 How long, LORD? wilt thou hide thyself for ever? shall thy wrath burn like fire?

47 Remember how short my time is: wherefore hast thou made all men in vain?

48 What man *is he that* liveth, and shall not see death? shall he deliver his soul from the hand of the grave? Selah.

49 Lord, where *are* thy former lovingkindnesses, *which* thou swarest unto David in thy truth?

50 Remember, Lord, the reproach of thy servants; *how* I do bear in my bosom *the reproach of* all the mighty people;

51 Wherewith thine enemies have reproached, O LORD; wherewith they have reproached the footsteps of thine anointed.

52 Blessed *be* the LORD for evermore. Amen, and Amen.

—LITURGY, LAMENT, ROYALTY, MESSIANIC

Book IV

PSALM 102

A Prayer of the afflicted, when he is overwhelmed, and poureth out his complaint before the LORD.

1 Hear my prayer, O LORD, and let my cry come unto thee.

2 Hide not thy face from me in the day *when* I am in trouble; incline thine ear unto me: in the day *when* I call answer me speedily.

3 For my days are consumed like smoke, and my bones are burned as an hearth.

4 My heart is smitten, and withered like grass; so that I forget to eat my bread.

5 By reason of the voice of my groaning my bones cleave to my skin.

6 I am like a pelican of the wilderness: I am like an owl of the desert.

7 I watch, and am as a sparrow alone upon the house top.

8 Mine enemies reproach me all day; *and* they that are mad against me are sworn against me.

9 For I have eaten ashes like bread, and mingled my drink with weeping.

10 Because of thine indignation and thy wrath: for thou hast lifted me up, and cast me down.

11 My days *are* like a shadow that declineth; and I am withered like grass.

12 But thou, O LORD, shalt endure for ever; and thy remembrance unto all generations.

13 Thou shalt arise, *and* have mercy upon Zion: for the time to favour her, yea, the set time, is come.

14 For thy servants take pleasure in her stones, and favour the dust thereof.

15 So the heathen shall fear the name of the LORD, and all the kings of the earth thy glory.

16 When the LORD shall build up Zion, he shall appear in his glory.

17 He will regard the prayer of the destitute, and not despise their prayer.

18 This shall be written for the generation to come: and the people which shall be created shall praise the LORD.

19 For he hath looked down from the height of his sanctuary; from heaven did the LORD behold the earth;

20 To hear the groaning of the prisoner; to loose those that are appointed to death;

21 To declare the name of the LORD in Zion, and his praise in Jerusalem;

22 When the people are gathered together, and the kingdoms, to serve the LORD.

23 He weakened my strength in the way; he shortened my days.

24 I said, O my God, take me not away in all the midst of my days: thy years *are* throughout all generations.

25 Of old hast thou laid the foundation of the earth: and the heavens *are* the work of thy hands.

26 They shall perish, but thou shalt endure: yea, all of them shall wax old like a garment; as a vesture shalt thou change them, and they shall be changed:

27 But thou *art* the same, and thy years shall have no end.

28 The children of thy servants shall continue, and their seed shall be established before thee.

—LAMENT, MESSIANIC

Below: God the Father by the Florentine sculptor Donatello, 1415: "For he hath looked down from the height of his sanctuary; from heaven did the LORD behold the earth" (Psalm 102:19).

PSALM 104

1   Bless the LORD, O my soul. O LORD my God,
    thou art very great; thou art clothed with honour
    and majesty.

2   Who coverest *thyself* with light as *with* a garment:
    who stretchest out the heavens like a curtain:

3   Who layeth the beams of his chambers in the waters:
    who maketh the clouds his chariot: who walketh
    upon the wings of the wind:

4   Who maketh his angels spirits; his ministers a
    flaming fire:

5   *Who* laid the foundations of the earth, *that* it should
    not be removed for ever.

6   Thou coveredst it with the deep as *with* a garment:
    the waters stood above the mountains.

7   At thy rebuke they fled; at the voice of thy thunder
    they hasted away.

8   They go up by the mountains; they go down by
    the valleys unto the place which thou hast founded
    for them.

9   Thou hast set a bound that they may not pass over;
    that they turn not again to cover the earth.

10 He sendeth the springs into the valleys, *which* run
    among the hills.

11 They give drink to every beast of the field: the wild
    asses quench their thirst.

12 By them shall the fowls of the heaven have their
    habitation, *which* sing among the branches.

13 He watereth the hills from his chambers: the earth is
    satisfied with the fruit of thy works.

14 He causeth the grass to grow for the cattle, and herb
    for the service of man: that he may bring forth food
    out of the earth;

15 And wine *that* maketh glad the heart of man, *and* oil
    to make *his* face to shine, and bread *which*
    strengtheneth man's heart.

16   The trees of the Lᴏʀᴅ are full *of sap*; the cedars of
     Lebanon, which he hath planted;
17   Where the birds make their nests: *as for* the stork, the
     fir trees *are* her house.
18   The high hills *are* a refuge for the wild goats; *and* the
     rocks for the conies.
19   He appointed the moon for seasons: the sun knoweth
     his going down.
20   Thou makest darkness, and it is night: wherein all the
     beasts of the forest do creep *forth*.

Left: Ezekiel's vision, as interpreted by Raphael, whose painting departs from the prophet's detailed description and appears rather to depict God as described in Psalm 104: clothed in light; riding a chariot of clouds; surrounded by angels; and creator of a pastoral earth and all manner of beasts.

21 The young lions roar after their prey, and seek their meat from God.

22 The sun ariseth, they gather themselves together, and lay them down in their dens.

23 Man goeth forth unto his work and to his labour until the evening.

24 O LORD, how manifold are thy works! in wisdom hast thou made them all: the earth is full of thy riches.

25 *So is* this great and wide sea, wherein *are* things creeping innumerable, both small and great beasts.

26 There go the ships: *there is* that leviathan, *whom* thou hast made to play therein.

27 These wait all upon thee; that thou mayest give *them* their meat in due season.

28 *That* thou givest them they gather: thou openest thine hand, they are filled with good.

29 Thou hidest thy face, they are troubled: thou takest away their breath, they die, and return to their dust.

30 Thou sendest forth thy spirit, they are created: and thou renewest the face of the earth.

31 The glory of the LORD shall endure for ever: the LORD shall rejoice in his works.

32 He looketh on the earth, and it trembleth: he toucheth the hills, and they smoke.

33 I will sing unto the LORD as long as I live: I will sing praise to my God while I have my being.

34 My meditation of him shall be sweet: I will be glad in the LORD.

35 Let the sinners be consumed out of the earth, and let the wicked be no more. Bless thou the LORD, O my soul. Praise ye the LORD.

—LITURGY, PRAISE

BOOK V

PSALM 108

A Song or Psalm of David.

Previous page: *The Psalms stress that only total obedience to, and devoted love of, God will bring spiritual happiness: "My meditation of him shall be sweet: I will be glad in the LORD" (Psalm 104:34).*

1 O God, my heart is fixed; I will sing and give praise, even with my glory.

2 Awake, psaltery and harp: I *myself* will awake early.

3 I will praise thee, O LORD, among the people: and I will sing praises unto thee among the nations.

4 For thy mercy is great above the heavens: and thy truth *reacheth* unto the clouds.

5 Be thou exalted, O God, above the heavens: and thy glory above the earth;

6 That thy beloved may be delivered: save *with* thy right hand, and answer me.

7 God hath spoken in his holiness; I will rejoice, I will divide Shechem, and mete out the valley of Succoth.

8 Gilead *is* mine; Manasseh *is* mine; Ephraim also *is* the strength of mine head; Judah *is* my lawgiver;

9 Moab *is* my washpot; over Edom will I cast out my shoe; over Philistia will I triumph.

10 Who will bring me into the strong city? who will lead me into Edom?

11 *Wilt* not *thou*, O God, *who* hast cast us off? and wilt not thou, O God, go forth with our hosts?

12 Give us help from trouble: for vain *is* the help of man.

13 Through God we shall do valiantly: for he *it is that* shall tread down our enemies.

—DAVIDIC, PRAISE

PSALM 110

A Psalm of David.

1   The LORD said unto my Lord, Sit thou at my right hand, until I make thine enemies thy footstool.
2   The LORD shall send the rod of thy strength out of Zion: rule thou in the midst of thine enemies.
3   Thy people *shall be* willing in the day of thy power, in the beauties of holiness from the womb of the morning: thou hast the dew of thy youth.
4   The LORD hath sworn, and will not repent, Thou *art* a priest for ever after the order of Melchizedek.
5   The LORD at thy right hand shall strike through kings in the day of his wrath.
6   He shall judge among the heathen, he shall fill *the places* with the dead bodies; he shall wound the heads over many countries.
7   He shall drink of the brook in the way: therefore shall he lift up the head.
    —DAVIDIC, ROYALTY, MESSIANIC

Below: Titian's David and Goliath *(1541) shows vividly the odds that the young David surmounted, with God's intervention: "The Lord at thy right hand shall strike through kings in the day of his wrath" (Psalm 110:5).*

PSALM 111

Below: In visual terms, this delicate Renaissance angel embodies the qualities of graciousness and compassion, verity and uprightness, which are attributed to God in Psalm 111.

1 Praise ye the LORD. I will praise the LORD with *my* whole heart, in the assembly of the upright, and *in* the congregation.

2 The works of the LORD *are* great, sought out of all them that have pleasure therein.

3 His work *is* honourable and glorious: and his righteousness endureth for ever.

4 He hath made his wonderful works to be remembered: the LORD *is* gracious and full of compassion.

5 He hath given meat unto them that fear him: he will ever be mindful of his covenant.

6 He hath shewed his people the power of his works, that he may give them the heritage of the heathen.

7 The works of his hands *are* verity and judgment; all his commandments *are* sure.

8 They stand fast for ever and ever, *and are* done in truth and uprightness.

9 He sent redemption unto his people: he hath commanded his covenant for ever: holy and reverend *is* his name.

10 The fear of the LORD *is* the beginning of wisdom: a good understanding have all they that do *his commandments*: his praise endureth for ever.

—THANKSGIVING, ACROSTIC

PSALM 113

1   Praise ye the LORD. Praise, O ye servants of the LORD, praise the name of the LORD.

2   Blessed be the name of the LORD from this time forth and for evermore.

3   From the rising of the sun unto the going down of the same the LORD's name *is* to be praised.

4   The LORD *is* high above all nations, *and* his glory above the heavens.

5   Who *is* like unto the LORD our God, who dwelleth on high,

6   Who humbleth *himself* to behold *the things that are* in heaven, and in the earth!

7   He raiseth up the poor out of the dust, *and* lifteth the needy out of the dunghill;

8   That he may set *him* with princes, *even* with the princes of his people.

9   He maketh the barren woman to keep house, *and to be* a joyful mother of children. Praise ye the LORD.

         —LITURGY, PRAISE

Below: Surrounded by infants, Leonardo da Vinci's Madonna of the Rocks *(c. 1480) vividly illustrates the joy of motherhood, as is described in Psalm 113:9.*

PSALM 114

Below: Michelangelo's The Creation of Adam (1508–12)— a detail from the ceiling of the Sistine Chapel. Although the Psalms celebrate God's miraculous powers of creation, they also warn of the perils of incurring his wrath: "Tremble, thou earth, at the presence of the Lord…" (Psalm 114:7).

1 When Israel went out of Egypt, the house of Jacob from a people of strange language;

2 Judah was his sanctuary, *and* Israel his dominion.

3 The sea saw *it*, and fled: Jordan was driven back.

4 The mountains skipped like rams, *and* the little hills like lambs.

5 What *ailed* thee, O thou sea, that thou fleddest? thou Jordan, *that* thou wast driven back?

6 Ye mountains, *that* ye skipped like rams; *and* ye little hills, like lambs?

7 Tremble, thou earth, at the presence of the Lord, at the presence of the God of Jacob;

8 Which turned the rock *into* a standing water, the flint into a fountain of waters.

—LITURGY, PRAISE

PSALM 118

1   Give thanks unto the LORD; for *he is* good: because his mercy *endureth* for ever.

2   Let Israel now say, that his mercy *endureth* for ever.

3   Let the house of Aaron now say, that his mercy *endureth* for ever.

4   Let them now that fear the LORD say, that his mercy *endureth* for ever.

5   I called upon the LORD in distress: the LORD answered me, *and set me* in a large place.

6   The LORD *is* on my side; I will not fear: what can man do unto me?

7   The LORD taketh my part with them that help me: therefore shall I see *my desire* upon them that hate me.

8   *It is* better to trust in the LORD than to put confidence in man.

9   *It is* better to trust in the LORD than to put confidence in princes.

10 All nations compassed me about: but in the name of the LORD will I destroy them.

11 They compassed me about; yea, they compassed me about: but in the name of the LORD I will destroy them.

12 They compassed me about like bees; they are quenched as the fire of thorns: for in the name of the LORD I will destroy them.

13 Thou hast thrust sore at me that I might fall: but the LORD helped me.

14 The LORD *is* my strength and song, and is become my salvation.

15 The voice of rejoicing and salvation *is* in the tabernacles of the righteous: the right hand of the LORD doeth valiantly.

16 The right hand of the LORD is exalted: the right hand of the LORD doeth valiantly.

17 I shall not die, but live, and declare the works of the LORD.

Right: Psalm 118 reminds the faithful that those who believe profoundly enough in God's mercy will overcome their tribulations: "The Lord is my strength and song, and is become my salvation" (verse 14).

Opposite: Titian's Penitent Magdalene (1567)—who found salvation through Christ—modestly covers herself in the presence of God: "I will lift up mine eyes unto the hills, from whence cometh my help" (Psalm 121:1).

18 The Lord hath chastened me sore: but he hath not given me over unto death.

19 Open to me the gates of righteousness: I will go into them, *and* I will praise the Lord:

20 This gate of the Lord, into which the righteous shall enter.

21 I will praise thee: for thou hast heard me, and art become my salvation.

22 The stone *which* the builders refused is become the head *stone* of the corner.

23 This is the Lord's doing; it *is* marvellous in our eyes.

24 This *is* the day *which* the Lord hath made; we will rejoice and be glad in it.

25 Save now, I beseech thee, O Lord: O Lord, I beseech thee, send now prosperity.

26 Blessed *be* he that cometh in the name of the Lord: we have blessed you out of the house of the Lord.

27 God *is* the Lord, which hath shewed us light: bind the sacrifice with cords, *even* unto the horns of the altar.

28 Thou *art* my God, and I will praise thee: *thou art* my God, I will exalt thee.

29 O give thanks unto the Lord; for *he is* good: for his mercy *endureth* for ever.

—LITURGY, PRAISE, THANKSGIVING, MESSIANIC

PSALM 121

A Song of degrees.

1   I will lift up mine eyes unto the hills, from whence
    cometh my help.
2   My help *cometh* from the LORD, which made heaven
    and earth.
3   He will not suffer thy foot to be moved: he that
    keepeth thee will not slumber.
4   Behold, he that keepeth
    Israel shall neither
    slumber nor sleep.
5   The LORD *is* thy keeper:
    the LORD *is* thy shade
    upon thy right hand.
6   The sun shall not smite
    thee by day, nor the
    moon by night.
7   The LORD shall preserve
    thee from all evil: he shall
    preserve thy soul.
8   The LORD shall preserve
    thy going out and thy
    coming in from this time
    forth, and even for
    evermore.

> —LITURGY, PRAISE,
> THANKSGIVING

Psalm 130

A Song of degrees.

1 Out of the depths have I cried unto thee, O Lord.

2 Lord, hear my voice: let thine ears be attentive to the voice of my supplications.

3 If thou, Lord, shouldest mark iniquities, O Lord, who shall stand?

4 But *there is* forgiveness with thee, that thou mayest be feared.

5 I wait for the Lord, my soul doth wait, and in his word do I hope.

6 My soul *waiteth* for the Lord more than they that watch for the morning: *I say, more than* they that watch for the morning.

7 Let Israel hope in the Lord: for with the Lord *there is* mercy, and with him *is* plenteous redemption.

8 And he shall redeem Israel from all his iniquities.

—LITURGY, PRAISE, LAMENT

Psalm 132

A Song of degrees.

1 Lord, remember David, *and* all his afflictions:

2 How he sware unto the Lord, *and* vowed unto the mighty *God* of Jacob.

3 Surely I will not come into the tabernacle of my house, nor go up into my bed;

4 I will not give sleep to mine eyes, *or* slumber to mine eyelids,

5 Until I find out a place for the Lord, an habitation for the mighty *God* of Jacob.

6 Lo, we heard of it at Ephratah: we found it in the fields of the wood.

7 We will go into his tabernacles: we will worship at his footstool.

8 Arise, O LORD, into thy rest; thou, and the ark of thy strength.

9 Let thy priests be clothed with righteousness; and let thy saints shout for joy.

10 For thy servant David's sake turn not away the face of thine anointed.

11 The LORD hath sworn *in* truth unto David; he will not turn from it; Of the fruit of thy body will I set upon thy throne.

12 If thy children will keep my covenant and my testimony that I shall teach them, their children shall also sit upon thy throne for evermore.

13 For the LORD hath chosen Zion; he hath desired *it* for his habitation.

14 This *is* my rest for ever: here will I dwell; for I have desired it.

15 I will abundantly bless her provision: I will satisfy her poor with bread.

16 I will also clothe her priests with salvation: and her saints shall shout aloud for joy.

17 There will I make the horn of David to bud: I have ordained a lamp for mine anointed.

18 His enemies will I clothe with shame: but upon himself shall his crown flourish.

—LITURGY, PRAISE, ROYALTY,
MESSIANIC

Below: Solomon, the son of David, was the builder of the First Temple, "an habitation for the mighty God of Jacob" (Psalm 132:5). In this painting by Raphael (1509), his wise judgement, demonstrated in the dispute between two women who claimed motherhood of the same child, is celebrated.

PSALM 137

1 By the rivers of Babylon, there we sat down, yea, we wept, when we remembered Zion.

2 We hanged our harps upon the willows in the midst thereof.

3 For there they that carried us away captive required of us a song; and they that wasted us *required of us* mirth, *saying,* Sing us *one* of the songs of Zion.

4 How shall we sing the LORD's song in a strange land?

5 If I forget thee, O Jerusalem, let my right hand forget *her cunning.*

6 If I do not remember thee, let my tongue cleave to the roof of my mouth; if I prefer not Jerusalem above my chief joy.

7 Remember, O LORD, the children of Edom in the day of Jerusalem; who said, Rase *it,* rase *it, even* to the foundation thereof.

8 O daughter of Babylon, who art to be destroyed; happy *shall he be*, that rewardeth thee as thou hast served us.

9 Happy *shall he be*, that taketh and dasheth thy little ones against the stones.

—LITURGY, LAMENT

Right: These mournful angels, worshipping the Lord through music, recall the anguish and faith of the Israelites during the Babylonian Exile, vividly evoked in Psalm 137.

PSALM 143

A Psalm of David.

1 Hear my prayer, O LORD, give ear to my supplications: in thy faithfulness answer me, *and* in thy righteousness.

2 And enter not into judgment with thy servant: for in thy sight shall no man living be justified.

3 For the enemy hath persecuted my soul; he hath smitten my life down to the ground; he hath made me to dwell in darkness, as those that have been long dead.

4 Therefore is my spirit overwhelmed within me; my heart within me is desolate.

5 I remember the days of old; I meditate on all thy works; I muse on the work of thy hands.

6 I stretch forth my hands unto thee: my soul *thirsteth* after thee, as a thirsty land. Selah.

7 Hear me speedily, O LORD: my spirit faileth: hide not thy face from me, lest I be like unto them that go down into the pit.

8 Cause me to hear thy lovingkindness in the morning; for in thee do I trust: cause me to know the way wherein I should walk; for I lift up my soul unto thee.

9 Deliver me, O LORD, from mine enemies: I flee unto thee to hide me.

10 Teach me to do thy will; for thou *art* my God: thy spirit *is* good; lead me into the land of uprightness.

11 Quicken me, O LORD, for thy name's sake: for thy righteousness' sake bring my soul out of trouble.

12 And of thy mercy cut off mine enemies, and destroy all them that afflict my soul: for I *am* thy servant.

—DAVIDIC, LAMENT

PSALM 150

1 Praise ye the LORD. Praise God in his sanctuary: praise him in the firmament of his power.

2 Praise him for his mighty acts: Praise him according to his excellent greatness.

3 Praise him with the sound of the trumpet: praise him with the psaltery and harp.

4 Praise him with the timbrel and dance: praise him with stringed instruments and organs.

5 Praise him upon the loud cymbals: praise him upon the high sounding cymbals.

6 Let every thing that hath breath praise the LORD. Praise ye the LORD.

—LITURGY, PRAISE

Right: "*Praise him with the sound of the trumpet...*" (Psalm 150:3). The psaltery, harp, timbrel and cymbals have all been depicted in the hands of angels, but the trumpet has a special significance in Judeo-Christian belief, for it summons the faithful to worship.

GLOSSARY

In the King James Bible, italics indicate words accented or stressed for poetic rhythm.

Aha, aha: Believed to be a confirmatory expression.

Aijeleth Shahar: From the Hebrew *ayyeleth hash-shahar*, "the hind of the morning." Generally interpreted to mean "help in the morning."

Alamoth: Hebrew word meaning "virgins." A musical term variously believed to refer to female voices or musicians, or to a high-pitched, treble tone.

Al-taschith From the Hebrew *'al tasheth*, "destroy not."

Amen A Hebrew word expressing confirmation or assent: "It is so."

Asaph A Gershonite Levite (priest) who led the services of praise during the reigns of David and Solomon. Twelve Psalms bear his name. The Asaphites were Temple musicians and singers.

Bashan: An area of land east of Galilee.

Benjamin The son of Jacob and the name of the tribe that descended from him.

Cassia A plant used as an ingredient in the holy oil for anointing in the tabernacle.

Edom The descendants and nation founded by Esau; enemies of the Jews.

Ephraim The younger son of Joseph and grandson of Jacob; the tribe that descended from him and the lands they settled.

Ephratah From the Hebrew *'ephrath*, "fruitful land," often used in association with Bethlehem.

Ethan the Ezrahite A Temple musician appointed by David; also a wise man. "Ezrahite" equates to "Israelite."

Gilead An area of land east of the River Jordan.

Gittith The exact meaning of this word is unknown, but it is believed to be a musical term, possibly referring to "the instrument from Gath."

Heman the Ezrahite A Levite musician appointed by David; possibly the son of Zerah and grandson of Judah; also a wise man. "Ezrahite" equates to "Israelite."

Hermon From the Hebrew for "sacred mountain." A mountain on the border with Lebanon.

Indite: To compose or write.

Jah Short for *Jahweh*, the Hebrew word associated with God, whose true name could not be written or spoken.

Jordan The River Jordan, signifying entry into the Promised Land.

Judah The fourth son of Jacob; the name of the tribe that descended from him and of the lands they settled.

Lovingkindness A composite word derived from the Hebrew *hesedh*.

Mahalath A musical expression, possibly signifying "grief."

Manasseh Joseph's oldest son, grandson of Jacob; the tribe that descended from him.

Maschil From the Hebrew *maskil*, meaning "intelligent/attentive/instruction"; in the context of the Psalms, it is generally believed to be meditative or educational, but it could be a musical instruction relating to a special skill.

Melchizedek A priest-king of Salem (probably Jerusalem).

Michtam Believed to mean "an inscription slab"; possibly also a purification term meaning "to cover."

Moab Lot's grandson; the name of the tribe that descended from him and of the lands they settled.

Naphtali The son of Jacob and the name of the tribe that descended from him.

Neginoth Probably the name of a stringed instrument.

Ophir A land in southern Arabia famous for its gold.

Philistia The land of the Philistines.

Psaltery A musical instrument, believed to have been a form of four-sided zither with ten strings; the term can be associated with the Ten Commandments and the Gospels.

Rahab A mythical sea monster.

Salmon Probably a mountain in the Bashan region.

Shechem A city and area in Ephraim.

Selah From the Hebrew *salal*, "to lift up." Possibly a musical instruction indicating a dramatic pause, or a word meaning "always."

Sheminith A musical expression meaning "on the eighth," and referring either to an eight-stringed instrument or to a low voice or tone.

Shoshannim From the Hebrew, meaning "lilies." The exact meaning of its use in the Psalms is unknown, but it could refer to a musical instrument (such as a lily-shaped bell), or to songs of spring.

Sinai The mountain on which God gave Moses the Law; also the desert region where the Israelites went after leaving Egypt.

Song of Degrees Also known as "Song of Ascents" and including Psalms 120–34. It is believed that the degrees represent certain steps in the Temple, or the songs sung by pilgrims to Jerusalem.

Sons of Korah Korahites, descendants of Korah, son of Izhar, and musicians and doorkeepers in the Temple. There are 11 Korahite psalms.

Tabernacle The holy sanctuary that contained the ark of the covenant.

Tabor A mountain of Galilee, scene of a battle, of idolatrous worship and later of the traditional site of Christ's Transfiguration.

Tarshish An ancient country of uncertain location, mentioned in I Kings.

Timbrel A musical instrument akin to a tambourine.

Tyre A rich Phoenician port.

Valley of Baca From the Hebrew *bakha*, "a balsam tree"; also translated as "Valley of Weeping."

Valley of Succoth A depression in the Jordan Valley.

Zebulun The son of Jacob, and the name of the tribe that descended from him.

Zion One of the hills on which Jerusalem was built, and upon which David installed the Ark of the Covenant, making it a sacred place. Synonymous with Jerusalem and with the Jewish religion.

Ziphims/Ziphites: Of the town of Ziph, near where David hid from Saul.